To, D.

with love +
Best wishes
Nutan

MW01251932

ZINDAGGI

From India to the Heartland

To;

Dearest Melissa

with love +

Best wishes

Taylor

ZINDAGGI

From India to the Heartland

A MEMOIR OF FAITH & FAMILY

BY NUTAN PHILLIPS

TATE PUBLISHING & *Enterprises*

Published by Tate Publishing & Enterprises, LLC
127 E. Trade Center Terrace | Mustang, Oklahoma 73064 USA
1.888.361.9473 | www.tatepublishing.com

Tate Publishing is committed to excellence in the publishing industry. The company reflects the philosophy established by the founders, based on Psalms 68:11,
"The Lord gave the word and great was the company of those who published it."

Book design copyright © 2007 by Tate Publishing, LLC. All rights reserved.
Cover design by Lindsay Behrens
Interior design by Jennifer Redden

Published in the United States of America
ISBN: 978-1-60274-540-3
07.05.02

INTRODUCTION

This is a book about my life experiences and what they have taught me. My story includes my transformation from an immature young Indian girl to a grown woman, the clash of cultures and traditions between my native country and my adopted home, and the long process of finding my identity and growing closer to God in the process. I pray that people will learn from my experiences as I have—that just because you love someone completely it does not mean they will love you back in the same way, or that when they do learn to love you in that way, you will be ready to accept it as reality. Life is short and precious, and it goes by so quickly that we often forget it is all about love, everyday forgiveness, and letting go. As the Bible says, we should not let the sun set on our anger or let resentment build towards anyone. There is no time for that. It seems like yesterday that I was holding my beautiful baby boy in my arms in the hospital, and today he has graduated from high school.

I believe that families are worth fighting for. Children

should have both a mother and father at home to give them the best chance of growing up well adjusted and loving. Young people considering marriage should begin to pray about their future family and continue to pray every day throughout their lives that God blesses that family. We can get caught up in the shortcomings of other people, or be so focused on our own needs that we can't see the needs of others. In order for relationship to last and grow, we must forgive over and over again and refuse to live in the past. There is always hope and new possibility for people who love one another and are committed to making relationships work.

There is one more chance for the human race, and I truly believe in it, that the future generations will learn to love and believe in the power of love. If I am not around to tell my story, they can read this book and know that love survives all odds if we forgive and let go. Surrender to God; His love is the only way.

This book is dedicated to Carmen and David, the loves and infatuations of my life, through whom God has taught me the meaning of unconditional love and showed me the purpose for my coming to the United States. It was not because of my ambition, or because I wanted to experience the freedom a woman can have here, but to give birth to these precious children and raise them for God. I know that all I have experienced was planned by Him before I was knit together in my mother's womb (Psalm 139:13) and that once I have surrendered to His plan, my years will be happy and fulfilled. Praise God for miracles, both big and small.

Please enjoy my story and send me your comments.

Nutan Mehtani Phillips

CHAPTER 1

I grew up in a small town in India called Bilaspur. The closest cities to us were New Delhi and Bombay, but the culture where I lived was still conservative, not yet influenced by the western elements creeping into the bigger cities. As far as I remember, my family was dominated by my mother, who was very strict with us. Young girls were to be seen and not heard and were to unconditionally accept the wishes of their parents with respect. The idea of a child speaking to an adult with disrespect or in rebellion was unheard of, and this type of thing just did not happen. I was trained at an early age to watch my words, control my mouth, and defer to the decisions of those who knew better. I had four siblings, two brothers and two sisters, and I was the oldest of the girls. We learned to speak both Hindi and English growing up and were fortunate to be educated, since most females at that time were not.

My memories of childhood are predominantly the good ones—the family attending church together every Sunday, going to the movies, eating meals together, praying with my parents, or visiting family friends. We did not have TV until 1980, when I was twenty-two years of age. There was very little outside cultural influence in my young world, and I grew up with East Indian beliefs, morals, perceptions, and conventions.

My mother was a strong woman with many leadership qualities. She was very active and involved in our church, which was a Christian church in the village. In India there is the Catholic Church, the Hindu faith, and Christian believers. There are not the various denominations that exist in American religious society, just churches of certain faiths. I attended many Christian conferences and conventions with my mother and recall falling asleep at most of them, especially the revival meetings. Occasionally, my mother would travel to other countries for these conferences, and it was at a Disciples of Christ International Convention in Adelaide, Australia, that she met her friend Ivy from North Carolina in the United States of America. This friend of my mother's would become a central figure in my adult life and the key to my relocation from India to the U.S. She was known to me as Aunt Ivy and was the godmother of my youngest sister, who was her namesake.

I have three siblings, and they are my older brother (Shailendra) and two younger sisters (Swati and Ivy). I was fourteen years old before my younger sisters were born, so I had grown accustomed to my parents' time and adoration. I was their only girl for so long, and they went as far as moving our family to Jabalpur while I attended school there. They wanted to be sure that I was formally educated and taught to read, speak, and write English by the nuns who ran the Catholic school. Both my mother and father worked very hard to support our family and give the four of us as much opportunity as possible. They were educated people and they believed in education. During the two years I was at the Catholic school in Jabalpur, my family experienced some major changes and hardship.

My father was a physician, a doctor, holding the equivalent of an M.D. degree. Because we lived in a small town and my father ran a clinic there, he did not make an extravagant living. He was like the "town doctor," helping the people to stay as healthy as possible. In India there is no health insurance system, so people who were unable to pay for my father's services would often come to the clinic. He was a kind and generous man who was known for his desire to help his patients, even if it came to giving them a hot meal or some clothing to wear. When our family moved to Jabalpur for me to attend school, my father was forced to start up a new clinic in a new place. This one was not as successful as the clinic in our hometown, and my father had a hard time building a patient base and rapport with the people there. As soon as I was finished with school, we moved back to Bilaspur.

Before we lived in Jabalpur, my mother became pregnant with my baby sister, Swati. My mother always worked outside the home and was a very busy, industrious woman. She was educated as a teacher but mostly helped my father in his clinic. She became like a doctor herself, although she had no formal education in that area. She would give vaccinations, medications, first aid, and medical advice to my father's patients. Due to the differences in the health care system, my mother did not have to be licensed and insured like she would have to be in the U.S. Basically, my mother might as well have been a doctor herself.

With the return to Bilaspur, my mother was busier than ever with her work and the new baby. I became jealous and resentful of my sister. Very often I was her caregiver, although we did have a nanny in our home, along with other servants. This was not uncommon where I grew up. I wanted to make sure my baby sister was well cared for, but resented the time it took away from my life. Because of the upheaval of moving twice in two years, the failure of my father's clinic in Jabalpur, a new baby, and my teenage years setting in, there was a lot of tension and stress in the household. My older brother was rebelling and having serious personal problems. All of us were emotionally spent and tired.

In 1974, my parents went to the United States to visit good friends in New Bern, North Carolina. My mother had met Ivy Chadwick through the Christian church, as I mentioned, and they kept in touch long distance. At this time my sister, Swati, was eighteen months old and was left in my care during my parents' absence. I was more like a second mother to her than a big sister. At the time of their travel, my mother was pregnant with Ivy Mary, my youngest sister. While my parents were in North Carolina, my new baby sister was born. The local newspapers covered the story, and my parents received a lot of attention from the Americans. Several articles were written about their trip from India to the U.S., and a sharing of customs occurred in the community. It was decided that my sisters and I would visit Aunt Ivy as soon as enough money could be saved to fly us from India to North Carolina. The cost of the airline tickets was always the stumbling block for our family, who loved the United States and wanted to visit regularly but simply could not afford it.

During the next few years, I attended Bombay University and earned a bachelor's degree in science and then a master's degree in sociology. I was a hard worker and had a very competitive spirit. Right after my graduation from college, I began to work for King Edward Memorial Hospital as a full-time social worker. The job involved long hours and a lot of interaction with people, and I appreciated the challenge as well as the pay. After my parents' financial struggles that started in Jabalpur, I was determined not to make the same mistake about money. I would remain in a secure, good-paying position, I was determined. I would help support my immediate family and also make a good life for myself.

At this time, I was still living at home. In my culture there is no "age of adulthood," like the magical age of eighteen in American culture. Families typically live together perpetually, as parents age and pass on and the children become the grandparents. The family always takes care of one another, shares a home, grows together. I could foresee this life for myself and would have been happy there where I was born and raised, but God had other plans for me. I had a dream of going to the U.S. and earning money to send home to my family. I saw the United States as the land of opportunity, literally. I was fairly unaware of the major cultural differences and completely idealistic about what my dream-life would be like there.

Of course, that is not all I was dreaming about in my future. Like most young girls, I had formulated the image of my perfect man, the one who would become my husband and take care of me for life. He would be a Prince Charming, strong and handsome, and we would be together forever. In my culture, the divorce rate is very low (about three percent when I was growing up, and about ten percent now) because we believe that the first love is the only one. Through sharing life together, man and wife grow to love each other more and more deeply and commitment is total. These are truths that are not tested in my society, and the thought of reciting vows without meaning them is unheard of. Lying about something so serious would be completely foreign to an East Indian.

When I was of marrying age, roughly ninety-four percent of marriages in my country were still arranged by the parents of the daughter. They would select a young man who seemed promising as a husband, usually with the help of a priest or pastor. The girl's parents would speak to the prospective mate's parents, and the engagement would take place. Oftentimes, the bride and groom had not met until their wedding day, although sometimes they were allowed a few chaperoned dates prior to marriage. The Indian belief is that a person loves and marries only once in life for life ("Pyar sirif ek bar hi kiya jata hai Jindigi me"). Although today there are so-called "love marriages" in India that are not arranged, about eighty-four percent of them still are. Another difference between marriages in the two cultures is that the bride's family is responsible for paying a sizable dowry in most Indian betrothals. The bride's family also pays for all wedding expenses, all jewelry, food, and lodging for the sometimes-large Indian families who come as guests. It is well known that funding a *Suhagrat* wedding is an expensive matter.

From the time I was a child I dreamed of such a wedding, with me dressed in beautiful wedding clothes and the object of this huge celebration.

As you can see, as I reached the age of maturity and completed my education, became a professional, and helped to take care of my sisters and family, I became confident that I was going to move mountains. No matter where I ended up, everything would be perfect, just like I had it planned. Sure, I was scared about the possibility of traveling as far away as across the ocean, far from everyone and everything I knew and loved, but more than scared, I was excited. My future seemed bright and the possibilities endless.

CHAPTER 2

Little did I know at the time, but my life was to change drastically in 1984 when I visited the U.S. for the first time. It was then that I, along with Aunt Ivy, began to discuss the possibility of me coming to the United States permanently. Prior to that time, I was like most Indian young women, wanting to help support my family and also wanting to get married. It was assumed that this would all occur under my parents' roof, or at least under their guidance. They did try to arrange marriage for me, but when I met the prospective husbands, I kindly declined the offers. I was in my twenties, and most Indian young women are married by then. My parents were anxious for me to find the right husband before becoming an "old maid," as they call it here. I was not overly anxious to be married but wanted badly to please my parents and trusted them to know what was best. I was also aware that they would be required to pay a sizable dowry when I married. Traditionally in my country, the bride's family pays for every expense involved in hosting the wedding ceremony and celebration as well as making payment to the groom's family. The bride's parents are also responsible for buying gifts for everyone taking part in the ceremony, often jewelry, and paying to lodge the many relatives that migrate to the area when a marriage takes place. This becomes an expensive proposition, and I was concerned about my parents' ability to come up with that kind of money. I suppose I was hoping to help with those costs when the time came.

Putting aside all of these concerns, I jumped at the chance to travel to America when it came in the year 1984. Ten years earlier during my parents' visit to New Bern, Aunt Ivy was named as my youngest sister's godmother. Little Ivy Mary Mehtani was born in the U.S. during that visit while I was back at home in India watching after Swati and the household. The older Ivy was anxious to see her godchild and to meet my sister and me, and she saved money for years to be able to send us three tickets to come visit. By this time Aunt Ivy was in her eighties and living alone in New Bern, North Carolina.

When my sisters and I traveled abroad to the U.S. that year, I was twenty-six, Swati was twelve, and Ivy was ten years of age. We stayed for three months in New Bern with Aunt Ivy, whose husband, Robert, was deceased. We also met and got to know her brother, whom we called Uncle Andrew, her daughter, Murri, and many of her friends from the Disciples of Christ church where she was a member. We visited Washington D.C. and the North Carolina coast, happily taking in the new sights and experiences. Aunt Ivy was a gracious hostess, and although she did not have a lot of money, she showed us a wonderful time. She relished having three young girls in her home, especially since we doted on her so. She became our adopted gandma, and that's what we called her.

Ivy Chadwick was born in 1903 and had a lifelong career as a schoolteacher. She was a down-to-earth, levelheaded, fun-loving woman who could put things in simple terms. I felt that she was easy to talk with and loved her right away. Ivy was married twice and had one daughter, Murri Chadwick, and two grandchildren. Her second husband, James Chadwick, died before we had a chance to meet him. Aunt Ivy never had a lot of money to speak of, but to us she was rich. I realize all these years later that she was probably living on her pension from teaching school and whatever pension of James Chadwick she was receiving, plus Social Security. Her home was modest but clean and well cared for in contrast to the homes in India, which are generally in bad repair and nothing to look at. Her yard was large and beautiful, with lots of pine trees, flowers, and grass. I recall that she had a grape arbor, and when we visited, the grapes were ripe on the vine. It was a special treat for us sisters to run outside to the grape arbor and pick and eat the fruit fresh off the vine.

Everywhere we went, my sisters and I dressed in formal *Saris,* or dresses with wrap-around shawls. Our deeply colored fabrics and Eastern appearance seemed to fascinate the local North Carolinians, as would the classical Indian dance poses that my sisters and I would perform. Because I was already a young adult and had a better command of the English language than my sisters, I did most of the talking and explaining about India. There were so many differences between Indian and American culture that we were fascinated and enthralled.

The friendliness that the local people showed us and each other was refreshing coming from India, where people seem far too busy to involve themselves with the lives of others. Of course, the television programs were new to us, too, and we loved to watch sitcoms that made us laugh. (In my country the television is run by the government, and there are not many shows to choose from). Among our favorite shows were *M*A*S*H* and *Three's Company*. We had our first hot dogs and hamburgers, fresh crab, peanut butter, and barbeque. The three of us were fascinated with the American diet, which was drastically different from the food we grew up eating in India. We were surprised at the number of restaurants and amount of "eating out" that the Americans enjoyed, since that was not part of our life back home. We were also surprised at the quantity of food the Americans ate, especially when it came to meat. In India, only a small portion of meat is served with each meal, whereas in America the meat is the main course.

A drastic difference that we noticed between India and America involves the cleanliness and garbage handling. In my country, people throw their trash wherever they like, whether in the streets or their yard or on the floor or in the roadway. Pretty much everywhere you look there is garbage. My sisters and I were impressed with the number of garbage cans everywhere, designating where to put your garbage! The roadside pickup of the cans each week was also a source of amazement, as well as the beautifully landscaped public properties and private yards. Back home in India there are not many flowers to look at, and in general it is overpopulated, crowded, and dirty. America was truly beautiful to us.

A very special thing happened while we were at Aunt Ivy's, which was that her nephew, Robert, and his second wife came to visit. Robert was Uncle Andrew's son. I recall that Robert was wearing white shorts and a white tee shirt the first time I saw him and was an attractive, friendly man. His wife was wearing the same thing, and it struck me as interesting that they dressed alike. I had no idea that he would play such a central role in my later life, but very much enjoyed meeting him because he was related to my dear Aunt Ivy. Robert invited us to come to Florida, where he lived and worked as an engineer, and go to Disney World. He talked of the fun things we could do there in Orlando and it sounded like heaven. Unfortunately, we were to travel back to India before our Visas ran out and did not have the opportunity to take him up on his offer.

When I returned to my country, I went back to work at Kind Edward Memorial Hospital again as a social worker, having taken a sabbatical during my months away. I was determined to get back to America but had to save up the money to get there. My job paid well, but I was also helping to support my whole family as I had intended. My work involved being on-call a lot, including weekends, and was very time consuming. I was gaining valuable experience but did not have time for social engagements or anything besides work and family. My sisters were older and needed help with schoolwork and looking after, which largely was my responsibility, as my parents were working full time too.

All the while, I kept in mind my desire to return to America and attend Chapel Hill College to earn a doctorate in Sociology. There, I would surely meet a Prince Charming and, like Cinderella, I would live with him happily ever after in the land of opportunity. My impression was that everyone in America was rich, since my native country is very poor, and I was exposed to this poverty on a daily basis. I was also convinced that Americans were smarter, in general. It seemed there was so much technology and organization in the United States. I dreamed of living in this place of intellect and monetary wealth, making my contribution as a social worker and living out a fairy tale at home with my perfect husband. My dream would be complete and my life fulfilled if I could just save up enough money for the ticket to America! This became my goal, and in 1986 I moved to the United States with nothing but my clothing and twenty dollars in cash. I was scared but excited, lacking resources but determined, an adult in years but extremely naïve. I came to America to find the ideal life and had no concept at all of what I would find instead.

CHAPTER 3

It was May 20, 1986, when I flew across the world to make a new home in America. I had many dreams of financially supporting my family with the money I would make in the U.S., plus making a life for myself in the land of opportunity. Initially, I stayed with Aunt Ivy and planned to apply for the doctoral program at Chapel Hill University in North Carolina. I had come from India with a tourist Visa and was hopeful that I could convert it to a student Visa without too much trouble. Once I was a registered college student, I would be allowed to stay in the U.S. and study until the completion of my degree.

My plans were interrupted when one day, out of the blue, Aunt Ivy's nephew, Robert, showed up at her house. I had met him briefly in 1984 when he had visited with his now ex-wife. Apparently, they had divorced in 1985, and Robert was visiting alone. To me he looked like Prince Charming, dressed in tight blue jeans and a white tee shirt. He was driving a "Z" sports car, worked in Florida as an engineer, was older, and appeared to have it all together.

Ivy began to explain to Robert my situation, regarding my Visa and my plans to go to college so that I could stay in America. She joked that unless I found someone to marry, I would need a student Visa to stay past three months. Robert replied, "I'll marry her!" and we all had a good laugh about it. I now realize the foreshadowing in that statement, and how little we both realized what we were getting into. But for the time being, it seemed like the most logical and appealing option.

Robert and I began to date while he was visiting in New Bern. We all went together to the Phillips family reunion for which he had come, he took me to the airport to watch the planes come and go, and escorted me around the area. One night we got a motel room in Havelock City where no one would know us. Robert asked me to take my clothes off and lie in bed with him. I had never done that before and I was nervous, but I liked Robert so much and wanted to please him so badly that I undressed and lay beside him. I was completely infatuated with him at that point and drank in the warmth of his body next to mine. We did not have intercourse that night, but instead explored one another's bodies and enjoyed the touching.

Robert understood that I was from a Christian background and also that I was fairly young, twenty-six years of age at the time. Robert was forty-three and had much more experience with these things than I. He kidded that Aunt Ivy would kill us if we were found to be messing around, so we went home late at night and slept in separate bedrooms, being careful not to be "caught." The next morning I went to wake up Robert and he said, "Let me get up, I don't have any clothes on," to which I started blushing. I waited for him in the kitchen, and when he came out of his room he took me into his arms and kissed me, held me, hugged me tight. He took me out to breakfast at Bojangles, one of the first places I "ate out" in this country. It still amazes me how often Americans eat out, based on my experience in India. It was Robert's favorite restaurant to eat breakfast at in North Carolina. After breakfast, he insisted that he was going to teach me to drive.

Robert was an amazing escort, a capable tutor, and a responsible chaperone for me. He taught me about U.S. culture, and he taught me how to drive. He took me to a large, empty parking lot so that I could practice. After a little driving, we stopped the car and began to make out in the parking lot. I had never felt this much passion and desire for anyone as I felt for him at that moment. I only learned a few driving skills that day, but I learned multitudes about how to kiss the American way. In India, people do not kiss on the lips, even in the movies. I never saw my parents kiss like that and had never been kissed before. It was extremely enjoyable with Robert.

It was at this time that I realized something very important—that I wanted to be a virgin when I got married, and that I wanted to be one man's wife and one man's only. I was convinced that I had found my man and was intoxicated by the attention he paid me. Robert was so knowledgeable and confident about everything—he was amazing in my eyes.

It was time for Robert to leave and return to Florida in a couple of days. I was devastated and didn't know how I could go on without him. My heart had completely forgotten about getting a Ph.D. and was captured by wanting to spend time with this desirable American man. Not only was my biological clock ticking, but everything seemed meant to be. During the time that I was in India between my two trips to America, I had formed a relationship with God and had been water baptized. I was trying to trust Him with my life and had prayed for my Prince Charming. I felt that this was God's blessing for me and an answer to prayer.

Robert wrote me letters from his work on his lunch hour, and we spoke on the phone every single night. He sent me flowers on my birthday, which no one had ever done for me before. It was a special occasion, and I was extremely excited. After a few weeks, he returned to North Carolina for his class reunion. On his way there, he got a speeding ticket and blamed it on me, saying that he was too anxious to see me. Of course, all of this flattered and encouraged me, especially because it was all so new. The night he arrived, we took blankets and pillows and went behind the small airport near Aunt Ivy's. It was a beautiful night, clear and romantic. We laid there and looked at the stars and then began touching each other again. Eventually, this became sexual touch and although we did not have intercourse once again, we satisfied one another in other ways. I knew by then that Robert was not just the love of my life, but also was my hero and was more than I had expected in a lover and would-be husband. I felt as if I was living in a movie, playing the starring role of princess, and I remember it like it was yesterday. My heart still yearns for that carefree, hopeful enthusiasm to return.

Robert had much going for him—he was working as an engineer for the space program, was an accomplished diver and excellent swimmer, a licensed pilot, chivalrous with women, and a fun-loving person. We went to his class reunion, and I met his ex-girlfriend and a lot of his friends from years before. People liked him and knew him there, and we had a good time. I believe I was introduced as his "friend." When the reunion was over, he returned to Florida. I mentioned to Aunt Ivy how many women came up to him at the reunion, and she made the comment, "Two good women left him, but women do seem to be crazy about him." It was hard to believe that Robert had been married and divorced twice, and I put that out of my mind.

Aunt Ivy, Uncle Andrew, and I decided to go to Florida for two weeks so that I could see where Robert lived. It was an unbelievable fairy tale time in my life as Robert showed us around Orlando. For the first time, I visited Sea World and Disney World and Kennedy Space Center. Robert's lifestyle was fascinating to me, as he took me to the movies, theaters for plays, restaurants like Red Lobster and a Japanese steak house, to the local bars, and to the beach. My memories of that time are very special, as I learned more about American culture and actually experienced it for myself. We went to the beach when we wanted some privacy and a chance to make out. Otherwise, if Aunt Ivy and Uncle Andrew were not in the condo, Robert and I would end up in the bed, going as far as we could morally go before marriage. It all seemed like a big dream, and I was head-over-heels in love. Every indication was that Robert felt the same, and the thought of parting with him again was

25

horrible, but I was at the mercy of others, since I could not yet drive, had no job, and was technically still just a visitor in the United States. When Aunt Ivy and Uncle Andrew decided to return to North Carolina, I would go with them. I prayed that Robert would marry me soon and longed for nothing but that sweet day.

CHAPTER 4

Just before we left Florida to return to Aunt Ivy's home, I recall that Robert mentioned to her that his sperm count was low and that if he married me, he knew I would want to have children. Aunt Ivy, in her matter-of-fact way, said, "It only takes one sperm to make a baby, Robert!" His mouth fell open and we all laughed at the joke. This was the first time there was a hint that Robert was having cold feet about marrying me, although he had said that he would. He had recently been divorced for the second time and wanted me to stay in Florida and get to know him better. However, in my culture I had been taught that a girl does not do this; she does not live or sleep with a man before marriage. Although Robert and I had been very physical with each other, we still had not had intercourse. As much as I wanted to, I believed that God's timing would bring us together when it was right. We returned to New Bern.

Aunt Ivy was getting concerned because my tourist visa was going to expire and she had no more finances to send me another ticket if I had to go back to India. A friend of hers suggested that in order to convert my visa, I should marry someone on paper and then when Robert was ready to marry me, I could legally divorce that person and marry Robert. I felt despair, and my heart dropped into my stomach. This was a horrible idea to me, and I couldn't believe my ears. I had no choice, for if I did not get married to someone, I would have to return to my country and never see Robert again. I had to take the chance that this crazy plan might work.

Aunt Ivy could not think of anyone who would marry me, not have sex with me, and then divorce me when Robert was ready to marry. It was a lot to ask of a man, especially knowing that I was in love with no one else but Robert. Aunt Ivy and Uncle Andrew decided that we should drive to South Carolina where no one knew us. Then Uncle Andrew would marry me on paper. That was the plan to keep me in America. My heart was crying inside of me—this was not how it was supposed to happen, not how it should be. I cried to God and thought of the beautiful wedding day I had dreamed of since I was a child. Like every girl, American or otherwise, I wanted the fairy tale. I had saved myself for my husband, protected my virginity, and now was ready to offer myself to Robert, but he wasn't ready to have me. I was eaten up with emotion but had to suppress all of it and try and be patient and wait for him.

I married Uncle Andrew in a small chapel in South Carolina. I remember that he kissed me on the forehead after the non-memorable ceremony. We returned to North Carolina that very same day, as if nothing had really happened. After a few days, we went to the immigration department in Raleigh.

They immediately knew that my marriage to Uncle Andrew was for the purpose of keeping me in the USA. Uncle Andrew tried to explain about Robert, and that we were just trying to give him time to make up his mind, and I just needed to stay long enough for that. The I.N.S. (Immigration and Naturalization Service) lady told Aunt Ivy that I would have to return to India as soon as we could have the marriage to Uncle Andrew annulled. I was crying, and Aunt Ivy was furious at I.N.S. over the whole thing.

All of the way back to Aunt Ivy's house I was thinking, *Oh, God, now I've missed my chance to marry my Prince Charming and no one back in India will marry me.* When I returned to my country, I would be in shame because of the false marriage to Uncle Andrew and the trouble with immigration services. It was possible I might even have a criminal record! Certainly no respectable Indian young man would want to marry me. I felt that everything was ruined and spoiled, but God knew the plans He had for me, to prosper and not to harm me (Jeremiah 29:11). He was transforming me into His image, and looking back I can see the purpose in my trials with Robert. However, at the time when all this was happening, I was crushed and confused.

Uncle Andrew contacted a law firm to get the marriage annulled, and they assured us that in a few weeks it would be all cleared up. I know that Aunt Ivy called and told Robert about the whole situation with I.N.S. and the marriage to Roy. I didn't hear the conversation, but when she was finished talking with him, Robert had agreed to marry me. Apparently, Aunt Ivy had given him money to go to college some years back, and they agreed that as a favor to repay her, he would help me to stay in America. Once the marriage annulment to Uncle Andrew was finalized, I was to go to Florida to be Robert's wife. The details of the arrangement didn't matter to me; I was just so happy to be able to stay in this country and be with my Robert.

Life seemed full of hope once I was on the Greyhound bus to Florida a few weeks later. It was October 2, 1986, and I was going to be with the love of my life. As soon as we reached Robert's condo, we made love. Yes, we could not contain our passion for each other, and we consummated the relationship. However, the next day Robert seemed confused about the marriage issue again. He mentioned that he just wanted to help me stay in the U.S. and then he was planning to divorce me once I had citizenship, which required five years of marriage. This broke my heart to hear him say that. What about our passion for each other? I reasoned that he was just angry with me for marrying his father without telling him. Certainly he couldn't be too happy about that. I was determined that when Robert saw and felt the love and commitment I had for him, I would win him back to me totally.

On Friday, October 10, 1986, Robert and I got married in front of a notary in the courthouse in Rockledge, Florida. I don't know about Robert, but when I took the oath of the marriage vows, I meant every word of it. Until death do us part, I was determined.

That night we did not make love. For some reason Robert was angry with me, and I felt all alone. Now I realize that he must have resented being forced into marrying me so soon. He had been dating a nurse named Susan before meeting me and had a social life and other friends here in his hometown. It was very confusing, because Robert was so physically attracted to me, and we were living as man and wife. I was learning to cook more American food, trying to learn from the neighbors how to live in this country. I rode the bicycle to the grocery store so that when Robert came home from work I had fresh meals ready for him. I was always ready to give him one hundred percent of myself, and was committed to the marriage and to satisfying him. However, Robert was hot and cold. Sometimes he would say that he wasn't ready to make love or didn't want to, while other times, we could hardly bridle our passion.

At some point, Robert told me that he wanted the freedom to date his other girlfriends and didn't want anyone to know about our marriage. He said that he had not told anyone at work that we were legally married and he wanted to keep it that way. Meanwhile, I wanted to tell the whole world! This marriage was my dream come true, and I wanted everyone to know how happy I was. I kept my mouth shut and did not question my husband.

I found a letter Robert had written to his girlfriend, saying how much he missed her and that his marriage to me was not real. He said that I was an Indian princess who wanted to have her way, but he really did not love me. When I read this, it totally broke my heart in pieces. It was like waking up from a bad dream; my love was so shaken for him. Fear came into my heart that Robert was definitely planning to leave me and that I would be all alone again. All that I believed was meant to be for me and for us seemed to be a lie. Robert told me to go out with other men and find someone to date—he even tried to fix me up with one of his co-workers! I was not interested in any of this—my heart belonged to him and only him. I was willing to make whatever adjustments necessary to be a good wife, but I wasn't going to start dating around.

Robert would always go out on Friday and Saturday nights. He would try to rent me enough movies to watch to help pass the time for me. This was humiliating, and my self-esteem was shot as a woman. I wanted to be everything to my husband, and here he was rejecting my love. How had I failed to be a good wife to him? Why did he not want me? Why did he feel the need to date other women?

One Friday night in March 1987, Robert invited one of his girlfriends over to the condo to have dinner. He asked me to remain upstairs, out of sight. Robert cooked a nice meal for this girl, and then they went in the living room. They were listening to music, dancing around, talking, and laughing. I didn't know how much of it I could take. I was trying to read but was basically sitting there crying into my book. Around midnight I realized that Robert and the girl had gone into the other bedroom and closed the door. Of course, I wasn't stupid, and I knew what was going on in there. I felt furious.

I left the house and started driving on A1A in Cocoa Beach. I wasn't a very good driver yet and forgot to put my headlights on. A police officer pulled me over and told me he had been following me the last two miles. He asked if I was aware that my headlights were off. I was devastated and didn't say much to him. He wrote me a fifty-dollar ticket that I could not pay and sent me on my way.

I had been attending the Cocoa Beach Methodist church and was headed there to pray. The church was locked but not the windows of heaven. I knew that God was awake to hear my cry. There in the parking lot, I reached out to God and requested him to please give me someone who would love and respect me. I poured my heart out to Him and let the emotion come out. Then I returned to the condo. Robert's friend had left, and he was doing dishes at two o'clock in the morning. For the first time, I looked into Robert's eyes with hatred. I felt betrayed and used, and I doubted our sexual intimacy. To me it appeared that Robert was just having a good time with me when he wanted sex—a girl fifteen years younger than him weighing 120 pounds with a flat stomach and good figure. This had not occurred to me before, because I believed in true love and gave myself to him out of that love inside me. I realized that Robert was not ready for any commitment with me, that much was plain. How he had treated me that night wounded my heart so badly that it took years and years of prayer to heal and forgive.

Daughter in red bandana top: Carmen and her million-dollar smile. Her outgoing, charming personality is beautiful.

My intelligent son, David Rajive Phillips. He is very handsome. He doesn't talk much, but he has a very good sense of humor. He is a man after God's own heart.

Carmen and David. They fight a lot, but they love even more.

Thank you, God, for my beautiful daughter.

David and Carmen enjoying the ocean in Melbourne Beach,
Florida. Carmen is a beach bug, while David is a sports fan.

A happy family! We are content and blessed
with who we are and what we have.
#192 Boardwalk Causeway, Melbourne Beach, Florida

CHAPTER 5

I came from a culture where love kicks in *after* marriage, which is literally a foreign idea in the United States. We have a saying in India, "Pyar sirif ek bar hi kiya jata hai Jindigi me," that means, "We only love someone this special way one time in our life." This commonly known phrase refers to the first love, the love of a lifetime, the one to whom you are bonded for life. This is exactly the way I have always felt about Robert, and I still believe that it applies to us as a couple. Regardless of our circumstance at any given time during our relationship, he was and will always be my first love.

Later that year, in March of 1987, after my trust in Robert had been shaken, I told him that I had missed my period that month and wanted to go to a clinic to be checked by a doctor. When the blood work came back from the lab, it was confirmed that I was pregnant. I was both thrilled and surprised about this and called Robert right away at work to tell him of the arrival of our baby. In his voice I could hear that he was not surprised, and he seemed happy to have finally fathered a child at the age of forty-three! He came home from work early, and we went out dancing and then to Denny's for dessert. This happy night was complete when we came home and made love. Many times afterward, Robert reported he enjoyed my body best when I was pregnant with our son. We were starting a family together, and we both glowed with the excitement of a little one in our future.

We talked about the baby. Robert expressed concern because one of his siblings was mentally deficient and he felt that our baby might be affected by the same handicap. From that day on I prayed in my heart for the baby's health. I also knew that Robert suffered from some mental anguish. As a child, he had been physically abused (literally beaten up) by his father and had been in counseling off and on for years. When he was in college, he took medication for manic depression. Robert has a history of trouble with maintaining long-term relationships, as evidenced by his previous marriages and many flings with women, and he continued in counseling throughout our marriage. My prayers were that our child would not suffer from either of our dispositions in any way and would be entirely healthy and happy. I was trusting God to answer those prayers, and He did.

In April of 1987, before the pregnancy was far enough along to show, we went for a holiday in Key West. It was an enjoyable time, as we camped out, went diving, made love in the tent, and ate at posh restaurants. Robert definitely knew how to have a good time and was an experienced diver. The weather was great, the Keys were romantic, and it was like a honeymoon experience.

After returning from the Keys to our Cape Canaveral condo, things began to go downhill. Robert started to speak of me having an abortion. This obviously disturbed me greatly, but I had no one local with whom to speak—no family or trusted friends in my new hometown. I had always believed in the Christian church and its ministry, so I went to speak to our pastor, who prayed with me and told me one important thing that struck me as the truth. He said, "If a man is not ready to be a father at age forty-three, he will never be ready." This empowered me to make a decision, and that day I vowed to have our baby with or without the support of my husband. This was a major leap of faith for me, and I have been greatly rewarded with two beautiful children who adore me and vice versa! They are blessed to have an understanding of two distinct cultures, and the three of us have a wonderful, growing relationship to this day.

About a month later, in May, Robert took me to Aunt Ivy's house and literally dumped me there. He had started to become physically abusive and mean towards me, and he insisted that I not return to him until I was willing to abort the baby. By then I felt like a lioness, ready to fight for my baby. The only way I can explain this, after letting others make my decisions for so long, was that God provided me with the strength to say what needed to be said. I told Robert that he was not allowed to make decisions for my body. By that time he had begun to threaten me with taking away my chance for citizenship, and I told him that I did not care, that I had faith that this child was

God's will, and I was going to have the baby even if it cost me my U.S. citizenship. We were both angry, especially Robert, but my mind was made up.

The next morning I flew back to Florida (with the help of Aunt Ivy) and asked my friend Patty from church to pick me up at the airport. She did, and I was able to reach the condo before Robert got home from work. I locked myself in my room and told him that he could not come in. He was furious at me for returning home so soon, unexpectedly, and then shutting him out. My behavior had changed, and he didn't like it. He also saw that I was not going to change my mind about the baby and was not going to allow him to bully me.

As a last resort, Robert decided to try to hide me and gave up on the idea of abortion. I was starting to show my pregnancy physically, and soon people would ask questions. Robert did not like the idea of having to explain whose baby was inside of me, so he moved me to a place in Edgewater, Florida. Meanwhile, he rented a room from one of his friends in Merritt Island so that he could maintain his identity as a bachelor. I was relieved that he had dropped the subject of abortion and was ready to make what I could out of an increasingly dysfunctional marriage and another new place to live.

I promptly got a job at Daytona Beach Community College as a part-time instructor. It was thrilling to be teaching in America at the college level, and I enjoyed the idea of working again and giving back to the community. I was feeling good and the baby was healthy, which made me happy. However, I was troubled by my relationship with Robert and felt that I was the one compromising an awful lot. I tried to tell myself that I had to be satisfied with whatever part of Robert's life he gave to me, but my perceptions were rapidly changing now that I had two lives to look after.

I began to doubt myself as a woman and was irritable at Robert for trying to maintain two separate lives. Every two to three days Robert would come to see me, but he had no respect for my time and was frequently hours late to show up. He would tell me he was coming at 6 p.m. and would then show up at midnight. As a result of his disinterest and neglect, I felt that I was not beautiful enough, not worthy of him, not sophisticated enough to be Robert's life partner. I started watching soap operas in the afternoon to learn some of the American woman's ways and become more like the women of this culture in which I was living. Although my eyes were slowly opening to the truth, God was merciful only to show me what I could handle at the time. I was suspicious of Robert and angry with him but was still convinced that if I could only be the best wife in the world, his mind and heart would change. It seemed that I was in constant conflict, loving and hating Robert at the same time. The picture of reality was forming before me, but I was hesitant to turn away from my fairy tale views.

On Friday, October 13, 1987, I had a serious argument with Robert. I recall thinking it was strange that it was Friday the 13, although I am not a suspicious person. The fighting started because I accused Robert of messing around with his girlfriend, Susan, the nurse who he had been dating off and on since before we were married. I did not know whether Robert had the right to see other women because of our unique circumstance—all I knew is that I was totally committed to him despite all that had transpired. We were married on paper for the purpose of my citizenship, yes. We were also married in our hearts, or so I believed. How could a wife allow her husband to date other women when all she wanted to do was to be the one to please him? When I left for work that morning at 7 a.m., I was highly emotional and upset. Apparently, I blacked out while driving in the middle of singing *Jesus Loves the Little Children* to my unborn baby. The next thing I remember, my car was headed into a ditch, and I had broken pieces of windshield glass all over me. The car behind me had stopped to help, and I still recall the lady screaming, "Oh my gosh, she's pregnant!" when she saw me sitting there dazed. Suddenly, I realized what had happened and that I was pregnant and was fearful that the baby had stopped moving. The ambulance came and took me to the nearest medical center, and a friend from church came to sit beside me and pray with me for the baby's safety. Later that evening, Robert finally came to visit me. Praise the Lord, the little life inside of me was unharmed.

I was restricted from driving until the baby was born, understandably, I suppose. I continued to teach at the college up until December 12, and then on December 13, cooked some meals and froze them, as suggested in the pregnancy class I had attended. During all of my first pregnancy, Robert came and went as he pleased, and I led my own life in Edgewater. We talked on the phone and kept in close touch but were not living as a man and wife in love with one another. I stayed busy and focused on my health and that of the baby.

On December 14, I went into labor, and Robert took me to the hospital. After twenty-seven hours of pains and a lot of pushing, I gave birth to a beautiful baby boy with lots of curly, black hair. We had picked out the name David for him, and I loved him immeasurably. The following day we were scheduled to go home from the hospital. I waited for Robert to come pick us up, as I had assumed he would. He did not come. Eventually, I called our pastor, who came and took the baby and me home. Upon arriving there, I saw that Robert had cleaned the apartment and had fresh flowers waiting there for us. This was a nice gesture, but I was still angry that he had not come to take us home himself. When I questioned him about it, he said he couldn't come because he had to work. How could he miss an occasion like this? I did not understand and felt that he had little care for me or his own baby at that point.

In May of 1988, when David was about six months old, I found a receipt indicating that Robert had been using an attorney from an office in Jacksonville. When I asked him what it was about, he said that he felt he had defrauded the government by marrying me, and he had hired an attorney to have me deported back to India. His plan was to keep the baby in the U.S. but to have me sent home. He had friends back in North Carolina who would raise the child, he claimed. Of course, I was appalled by this that he would even think such a thing as separating me from David. However, it seemed that when his request made it to I.N.S., they immediately denied it and put the idea to rest. Once again, God was watching over us.

Apparently, Robert had exhausted his other options, so he finally decided to tell his co-workers and friends that I was his wife and that David was his son. He began to treat me better, doing things that I asked, and finally treating me as his wife.

Now that others knew the truth, he was able to stop living the dual life of before and see us as his family, maybe. Still, the seeds of resentment and mistrust were in my heart and soul. Could I trust him, and did I still love him after all that had happened? I tried to give him another chance, and I knew that I would have to forgive him and love him with every bit of my heart if it was going to work.

Robert had scheduled a diving vacation with one of his coworkers in September of 1988. Before he left for his trip, he took me out to dinner at a Mexican restaurant. We were having a good time, and I was feeling confident that I looked beautiful that night. As soon as we got home, we could not control ourselves, and the next thing I knew we were in bed together. Little did I know it at the time, but our second child was conceived that night.

When Robert left for his planned excursion with his friend, I decided to go to North Carolina and visit Aunt Ivy, who was aging and who I had been missing. I very much wanted her to meet David and went to stay with her for just a few days. We were having a nice visit, and she loved David and found him beautiful, of course. Meanwhile, Robert came home early from his trip. When he didn't find us at home, he began calling around looking for me. He eventually called Aunt Ivy's house and found me there. He told me he was home, and he was flirting with me over the phone, saying how much he missed me and wanted to see and touch me. Needless to say, the very next day I flew back to be with him. It was the first time in over a year that I felt he was actually trying to be committed to me. Even with all I had suffered at his hands, I wanted badly to believe that he loved me as much as I did him, and I was willing to forgive him to try and make our marriage what I had envisioned from the start. A ray of hope shone in my heart, saying that perhaps the bad dream was over and we were going to pick up the pieces and give the story a happy ending.

A few weeks later, I found out that I was pregnant again. I told Robert about our second baby, and he was very happy. I remember that he said, "Make it a girl this time, okay?" and we had a laugh. As it turns out, that was God's will also, because our little daughter was growing inside of me.

CHAPTER 6

In April 1989, we decided to move into a two-bedroom apartment on India Palm St. in New Smyrna, Florida. While we lived there, Robert started giving me his paycheck to run the house and pay all the bills. He was in debt, having charged up his credit cards, and wanted me to help him stay on a budget. He had always been a lavish spender and enjoyed the finer things in life. I was happy for him to trust me with the finances.

In June 1989, we learned that Aunt Ivy had been hospitalized and was not doing well. I was very pregnant at that time, but we decided to make the trip to North Carolina and see her while she was still alive. Prior to then, Robert and Aunt Ivy had a falling out about our relationship. I had confided in her and told her all the details of his behavior, and she was not happy with how he had treated me. All the same, Robert took David and me to see her for one last time. I was so grateful to say goodbye to her, and it was as if she had waited for me to come, because the very next day she died.

We were already traveling home to Florida and did not get to attend her funeral services. A short time later, in July 1989, our beautiful girl named Carmen was born.

At this time in our marriage, Robert and I were extremely financially strapped. I took a part-time job as a substitute teacher and was also making some home health visits doing counseling. We had no nearby family to help support us and two children to feed. Even so, Robert helped me to save up enough money for my mother to come and visit us. She stayed with us that late summer and early fall, and it was a blessing to have her there. My mother got along well with Robert and had no hard feelings toward him. She had no basis, since I had not shared with her and my father the marital struggles I had experienced. I did not feel they would understand and was certain that they would blame me for any failures in our relationship. In my culture, it is the wife's job to keep the husband happy at home so that he does not feel the need to wander. Anyway, my parents had begun to think that I was past marrying age and were just glad that I had found a husband. Even better, they did not have to pay any dowry to Robert since he was an American. In their eyes, I had a great thing going. At times, I believed the same.

For instance, while my mother was visiting, Robert had to go to California on business for a couple of days. When he returned, he took me to Daytona Beach for the weekend. He had reserved us an oceanfront room with a balcony, and I remember sitting there sipping on wine. I was dressed in a low-cut, revealing gown that revealed, and after dinner when we returned to the room, Robert and I could not wait to remove each other's clothing and make love in the large bed. The next morning, I felt that I wished the night would have lasted forever. Certainly, time waits for no one. We spent the next day at the ocean, relaxing at the beach and forgetting our troubles. Robert spoiled me by taking me shopping at the Daytona Beach Mall for a new dress for his company Christmas party that year. I had never felt so fulfilled and happy in my life.

After three months, my mother left for India, and our free babysitting was over. Even worse, so was my help and companionship. I dearly missed my mother. It was October of 1989, and things started to deteriorate again. Robert began coming home at two or three o'clock in the morning, saying that he was working late. Understandably, I was suspicious. We started arguing more and more, and things became sour between us. We were fiscally broke and had two children nineteen months apart, which was enough to stress any marriage. I wanted to start making more money, so I revisited the idea of going back to work full time, applying for positions at home health agencies and hospitals. Later that year, I found a full-time position with a home health agency in Melbourne.

I remember that around the same time Robert invited some of his friends from work over for dinner. I had never met this couple before, and I could instantly tell that they did not like me. What had Robert said to them? For the whole evening they were treating me strangely and acting somewhat cold toward me. At that time, my best friend and confidante was Patty, my friend from church with whom I ran the youth group. She was about fifteen years older than me and like an older sister. I depended on her and enjoyed her company, and she had always been there when I needed her. Patty's husband traveled a lot, which gave us the opportunity to spend more time with one another. I confessed to Patty that I thought Robert was saying things behind my back that were unkind, and I told her about the dinner party. She said a certain thing to me about Robert that only he and I could have known. I realized that Robert had also been talking with Patty behind my back, and I was angry. She and I had a falling out, and I blamed Robert for it. It seemed that some of my suspicions were founded.

I was keeping a separate bank account with my own money in it. That made Robert nervous and upset, but I felt that it was necessary because I did not trust him. He had bad money management habits, and I secretly feared that one day he would just up and leave me. At this point in our relationship, my trust in him had eroded totally. I realized that in the beginning I had trusted him too much, depended on him too much when I should have been trusting in and depending on God first and foremost. "It is better to trust in God than in man" (Psalms 188:8). My deepest fear was that Robert was always cheating on me with another woman and would eventually leave me, and I was paranoid about how he spent his time. I became watchful of him and looked for proof to support my doubts.

I convinced Robert to move closer to my work, and in the summer of 1991, we went to live at the Plantation Club apartments in Suntree, Florida. It was then that I got overly greedy and anxious to make lots of money and build my financial empire in America. I was working all the time, even in the evenings, when Robert was home to watch the kids, which allowed us to save on babysitting costs. My first goal was to make as much money as possible, get us out of our financial debts, and accumulate enough wealth to help support my family back in India. Unfortunately, I had to sacrifice time with my family in order to accomplish that goal. Perhaps I was also running from my problems and stress at home. Looking back, I was unaware of all of Robert's needs that were consistently unmet, and when he went back to counseling again, I failed to see that he was crying out for help. There was so much stress on our marriage at that time, and I was too busy to notice what was happening all around me—my precious family was falling apart.

CHAPTER 7

The wake-up call came for me on December 19, 1991 when I came home after work at two p.m. and noticed that the kids were gone, presumably with Robert. I stopped to think but really had no idea where they could be. It was a windy, stormy day outside and we had planned to go out Christmas shopping that afternoon. Only five days were left until Christmas, and we had no presents for under the tree! I waited for them to return, making plans for the upcoming shopping trip. When a couple of hours had passed, I began to worry, and my heart grew heavy. I could feel that there was something very wrong, and I knew better than to doubt my intuition.

The next thing I did was to start making phone calls—to local hospitals, Robert's place of work, local relatives, and friends. No one seemed to have seen them or knew of their whereabouts. Robert's sister-in-law, Ann, and her husband lived in Cocoa Beach at the time, and she came to support me during the whole ordeal. At eight that night I received a call from the Orlando International Airport saying that my husband and kids were on their way to California. Upon hearing those words, I went into a state of shock and panic and immediately began screaming as loudly as I could, "He's running away with the kids! Don't let him go! He's taking them!" It all started to make sense, like the fact that Robert had grown a full beard and changed his appearance. Apparently, he had also changed his name and the kids' names on the airplane tickets. I later found out that Robert had purchased one-way tickets to California and had not packed or carried any luggage for the kids or himself.

Orlando Airport security officials were looking for a drug dealer. They wanted to see Robert's ID, but he refused to show it, probably knowing that the last name would not match his ticket. When he would not show his ID, he was pulled aside for further questioning. Praise God that He was watching out for me and my children, keeping us together by intervening that day. Finally, Robert was forced to reveal his true identity and had the officials call me to verify who he was. Of course, when they did, I had the opportunity to give my side of the story, to put an end to the nightmare promptly. The airport cancelled the tickets and told me to come and pick up the children right away. However, I was in no state to drive at my current level of anxiety. I was forced to trust Robert to bring the kids home to me. It was one of the hardest things I have ever done, and I believe that I literally prayed them home.

That day I had no compassion for my one-time Prince Charming. On the inside I felt like a mad dog, ready to attack for her pups, and willing to bite the man that takes a four-year-old boy and a two-and-a-half-year-old girl away from their momma. It infuriated me just thinking of it, and I could've killed him. I am sure that Robert had some important explanation or rationale in his heart, but I was not interested in hearing it. When he finally showed up with them at two that morning, they were asleep in the car. I ran to the door and knelt to the ground, thanking the Lord for bringing my children back to me.

The only thing that Robert said to me once we were inside the house was, "Look how dirty and messy this place is." I looked around and, yes, it was messy and dirty. A pang of guilt struck me for letting the house go so far and not even recognizing it. Robert's sister-in-law, who was still there, suggested that maybe a maid service would be good for us. Perhaps that would help us to focus on repairing our marriage, she thought. She didn't exactly say that, but in so many words and with looks she communicated it.

I simply looked at Robert and said, "Get your clothes and things together and move out." I knew in my heart that I was letting something precious die, but I could not trust him anymore. He had put me between a rock and a hard place, and it seemed that I was forced to choose between my husband and my kids. There was no way that I was going to risk losing my kids at any cost, and I knew that if Robert and I were not divorced and he took off with the kids again, I might lose them forever. I was terrified of that possibility, and although Robert did not want to divorce, I began the proceedings. Meanwhile, I applied for a legal restraining order on him for thirty days. Since it took four days for the restraining order to become effective, David and Carmen and I stayed with a friend temporarily. Robert was calling everyone we knew, looking for us, trying to track us down. By the time he did, the December 22, he was no longer allowed to come near us.

Robert began pleading with me to go to counseling with him and to take him back and work things out. He insisted that he did not want to finalize the divorce, but I had made up my mind. Without trust, what could our marriage be? We remained separated for the following six months or so, Robert living in Rockledge while I stayed in our Suntree home. In April of that year, I became an official United States citizen, and I remember going to a ceremony in Orlando where I took the oath of citizenship. My friend Patty, with whom I had been reconciled, accompanied me that day, and, ironically, Robert was not invited or involved. We were married in 1986 and stayed together until 1991, which was exactly enough time for me to be granted what he had wanted to give me from the start.

On July 20, 1992, our divorce was final. It was a sad day for me, because I never wanted my marriage to end in divorce and had never dreamed that it would. I felt all alone again, with none of my family close by, and Robert was free to date other women at last.

I sank into the role of the single mother, working full time while my kids were at a babysitter's, then coming home and feeding them, bathing them, and putting them to bed. The next day it all happened over again, and so forth and so on. Unbeknownst to me, I was depressed and getting overweight. I would eat for comfort, and sleep from eight p.m. to eight a.m. nightly. I missed Robert and realized what a big help he had been with the kids and around the house. It was hard and overwhelming as a single mother, and I never seemed to have a break or anyone with whom to share the burdens.

My prayer life pulled me through the worries of that time period. I was still attending church regularly and making use of the prayer room whenever Robert had the kids. His visits with the kids were on Tuesday and Thursday evenings from five to eight and also every other weekend. The fear of the three of them disappearing again still haunted me, and I would pray with the elders there in the quiet presence of God, trusting Him to keep Carmen and David safe and bring them back to me unharmed. When it was time for them to return, I watched by the front window of my home, and if they were so much as ten minutes late I began to get impatient. God brought me through that time, and Robert was responsible about his visitation days.

Although I did not trust him, I had to admit that I was still missing Robert. I missed our physical life, sharing the kids, doing things as a family, and being a part of his life. When some time had passed after the divorce, Robert and I started to see each other more. At first we would do things with the kids like going to parks or out to restaurants. Then we went to a family reunion together and decided to take a vacation together as a family. We were getting along great and enjoying watching the kids grow up right under our noses. One particularly memorable trip that we took was up to Sliding Rock in North Carolina. Robert and I sat and watched the kids playing in the water, laughing and joking with each other happily. At night we stayed in a rustic cabin in the woods, and Robert and I made love on the patio as the children slept. I could not resist him.

Through all of this, I was getting stronger and learning to know myself better. In 1993, I actually took both of my kids to Disney World in Orlando by myself. This was something I never would have done in the past, and here I was navigating a busy theme park with two young children! That same year, I reported to my lawyer that Robert was sporadic and often late with his child support payments. We worked together to arrange for income deduction through Robert's company, and it was a great blessing to me. I established a budget for the kids, and I carefully planned our spending while also trying to save a little. Robert noticed my increased self-confidence, I am sure of it. Perhaps that made me more attractive to him, I don't know. It certainly gave me a different perspective, knowing that I didn't *need* him to survive and that I could make a responsible choice about whether to be with him or not.

Somehow, Robert and I kept hanging onto each other despite our circumstances. In 1994, he filed for full custody of the children. When I heard this, I had to try to keep from laughing out loud. It was an obvious attempt at getting to me, and I prayed it away. Sure enough, his case never went anywhere and did not make it to court. That same year, my father was able to come and visit from India for a few months. He had always liked Robert, and they got along well. While my dad was there, Robert and I went on several dates, including a nice evening at the Strawberry Mansion in Melbourne. That night, Robert presented me with a ring and asked me to remarry him.

I was surprised by this, and not sure, so I told him that I'd have to give it some thought. It felt flattering to have his proposal, but something also felt wrong about it. Looking back, I suppose I had not forgiven him for the time he tried to fly off with our children. I wanted to be his wife and lover, but not at the sacrifice of my kids. In the end, I gave the ring back to him and told him I wasn't ready to remarry yet, which was the truth.

During the years that followed, there were other boyfriends for me and other girlfriends for Robert. We would always play little jealous games when one of us had a date. I believe that we both felt we were meant for each other and needed one another to maintain a semblance of family unity. We did not want to lose each other totally and tried to remain friends no matter what. Sometimes Robert would still come to spend the night, and we would make love like old times. As much as I enjoyed this, I felt guilty because we were not actually married, and I wondered what God thought of this peculiar arrangement between us.

In 1996, my mother, aunt, and uncle came from India to visit for a few months. It was great to see my mother at last—it had been so long since we were together! I had not seen her since right after David and Carmen were born, and we had a lot of catching up to do. Of course, the kids had both changed so much that my mother enjoyed getting to know them again, and we had a wonderful time together. Once again, Robert and I went on a date during her visit, and he offered me another beautiful ring, proposing like he had two years before. This time I did not think about it but returned the ring and told Robert I did not believe it would be a good idea. I had become a different person and had grown accustomed to my lifestyle, I suppose. However, I often regret the decision I made that night, because I could now have my family back together, my husband in my arms, my first love returned to me like the prodigal son of Biblical history. The pain of rejection, failure, and guilt would be no more, and my life would make sense once again. However, we can never go back or reverse time, unfortunately.

I found that I was missing India, not having been back there in years, and in 1998, I decided to take my children for their first visit abroad. When I discussed my idea with Robert, I asked him to go along with us, but he declined. This made me unhappy, because I wanted to share India with him, but also because it was expected that I would be traveling with my husband. Indian women do not travel around the world alone with their children. That just would not fit into my culture. Nonetheless, I went without Robert and the kids and I had a wonderful time. They were amazed and overwhelmed by the Taj Mahal, a gigantic spiritual center that dwarfs everything around it and inside of it. I can't help but believe that one day Robert would go there and see it with me, and I would love that day!

When we returned from our four-week stay in India, Robert was at the airport waiting for us. The first thing that the kids, who were around pre-adolescent age, told him was that there were no traffic lights in India and everyone just *goes!* Robert and I had a good laugh about that, and it was great to be reunited as a family. After my time in India, I was very anxious to be married once again. I had even begun to think of an arranged marriage while I was there, wanting the family stability that is so common in my country. When I told Robert about my determination, he responded by saying that we should move back in together and remarry. Since this was my heart's real desire, I immediately said yes. That was March of 1999, and the next few months were blissful, with the four of us under the same roof again.

Robert and I never did set a date for the wedding. I wish that one of us would have taken that step, but we were both serious procrastinators from way back. Here we were going on dates, making love, taking the kids to baseball, soccer, and music lessons. It seemed as if we were still married, and that's how we lived. But it never took place—we were too busy with life.

I was offered a job in my field at a reputable major hospital in the area. Working for a big hospital in the U.S. was a major challenge for me, and I started to work long hours to succeed at my job. I was on call between the hours of five p.m. and seven a.m. and often worked overtime in addition. Of course, this meant that we were making a lot of money, and that had always been one of my goals upon moving to America. Remembering back to that time, Robert was very good to me and would often clean the house before I came home, rub my tired feet at night, or bring the kids up to the Emergency Room to see me while I was working there on weekends. He was treating me well and trying hard, but I was blind to what he was going through. He needed more from me than I was giving him, once again, because I was spending most of my waking hours at work. Like before, I did not even notice.

To give us both a break from the insanity of our home life and provide some quality time together, Robert asked me to join him in New York while he was on a work assignment that summer. I went along with him, and we had the time of our lives, just the two of us. I remember Robert taking me out to dinner at a fancy restaurant and proposing to me for the third time, offering me a ring and everything. It was so romantic and unexpected! This time I told him that I didn't want an engagement; I just wanted to get married.

In November of that same year, my father came to visit us from India and stayed for three months. Our household was busy and chaotic, with both of us working full time plus overtime and trying to manage the kids' lives and activities. While he was with us, my dad became ill and had to go to the emergency room several times. Robert was great about taking care of him while I was at work, and he and my father got along well. By the time my father left to return to India in February of 2000, my relationship with Robert had deteriorated once again to the point where conflict and stress ruled the household. I was working thirteen days in a row without break and was so caught up in it that I was unable to see what was happening at home. I had no idea what was coming.

CHAPTER 8

On January 21, 1999, my mother died. When I had been to visit her just a year before, it was obvious that her health was declining. I remember being very glad that I had decided to go and see my family, because my parents were visibly aging. The worst part about my mother's death was that I did not even find out she was gone until several months after she had passed away. No one made the effort to call me, and I basically heard it through the grapevine of the extended family instead of from my father or siblings, as it should have been. This angered me at the time, but there was nothing I could do except let it go. My mother had a long life, and I was able to be with her while she was still able to be herself with me. For that I am thankful, and although I miss her, I know that she is in heaven with the Lord. That is the best consolation ever.

Robert and I decided to try counseling to help us strengthen our relationship. I was attending the Faith Fellowship Church in Melbourne, and we took advantage of the counseling services they offered. I was going to counseling myself, and Robert and I were also going as a couple. The Christian advice was very helpful, and I grew personally from the experience. However, Robert was not a Christian and was also sporadic about going to the counselor with me, so I am not sure how much it helped us as a couple. It seemed that we both knew we had problems, both knew that our relationship was not growing, but neither of us had the time or energy to do anything about it.

I will never forget the day of August 11. 2001, when the kids and I came home after school and work to find that Robert had moved out without telling us. All three of us broke down in tears. I remember Carmen saying, "What a jerk—he didn't even tell us!" and then erupting into tears. As it turned out, Robert had moved in with one of his co-workers and was renting a room from him.

I was in shock and felt completely responsible for his leaving. I begged Robert to come back. I tried to convince him to move back home and get married right away. He wanted us to go back to counseling, but I was afraid. What if the counseling didn't work? Did that mean that we were going to split up for good? That we were incompatible? That we couldn't resolve our differences? I was confused, having been through so much with this man, and yet not knowing what I could expect from him. Perhaps I should have taken a leap of faith at that time, trusting that it was God's will for me to be with Robert, and relying on Him to bless our marriage, but Robert was adamant, sticking to his guns about his decision to move out. His strong-willed nature took over, and I knew that he wasn't coming back . . . at least not right away.

My emotional state was so fragile that I eventually shut down. As before, I became depressed and stopped eating right. I remember that in the months following Robert's departure I tried to date a couple of men. One was a man from out of state who was recently divorced. He was very nice, but I was not interested in anything serious, and he was looking for companionship. I made the decision that we should go our separate ways. The other was a lawyer from Orlando, who was a smooth talker and very easy with his money. After just a few dates, he offered me a ring and tried to come on to me, wanting to have sex. I decided to write men off all together for a while.

It was at this time when I totally and unreservedly gave my whole heart to God and began to walk in His ways. This was a turning point in my life, as I studied the Bible to learn God's character and His will, learning to offer up my body as a living sacrifice to Him. Interestingly enough, I thought I was completely fulfilled walking with Christ. I trusted Him to bring me my husband back and restore my family if that was His will. Knowing what it meant to be a Christian, I realized that I had a lot of forgiving to do in my heart before God would bless me. I also needed to learn to watch my mouth and to do a better job of prioritizing my life, especially the people in it who were the most important to me. I focused on my own personal growth and mental health so that God could use me in the lives of those I loved.

I was not dating but men were attracted to me frequently who wanted to take me out. I am considered a very attractive and young-looking woman and even younger men were interested in me. However, what they did not realize is that inside

I had the mentality of a typical Christian Indian woman, who was still attracted to her ex-husband and, in spite of everything, wished to put her family back together and correct the mistakes I had made rather than blaming the circumstances. I was learning from preachers such as Joyce Meyer and T.D. Jakes what it meant to really love another person the way that God intends. Although I yearned to put into practice the things I was discovering, I remained shut down towards Robert and other men.

Over time, I resolved my hatred and anger towards Robert and found that I could love him unconditionally even though we were not together. He was still my Prince Charming and always would be, I suppose. Perhaps a second book or final chapter will someday be written in which we live happily ever after as it is supposed to be.

Meanwhile, in Robert's life there was also turmoil after our separation. In 2002, he lost his job and was unemployed during the next eight or nine months before getting a job at Wal-Mart. I am sure that he was depressed and in despair, although he wouldn't let me help him, and I'm not sure that I could have. Sometime that year that he hit Carmen during one of their visits. DCF became involved, but we managed to work things out peaceably. In 2004, Carmen (age fifteen) started dating a boy who I did not approve of, and I would not let her spend time alone with him. I suspected that he was into sex, and I knew that he was not a very good student. My assumption was that he was not a good influence on my daughter. Robert had none of these insights and would help Carmen to sneak behind my back and date this boy. Carmen started to feel that their dad was easier on her, and that she could do whatever they wanted while staying with him. Therefore, she liked being at his place more than at mine. She told us so, and in 2003, Robert filed for full custody of both the children.

This began a painful and tumultuous time in my relationship with my kids. On April 23 of 2005, Carmen and I had a bad argument, and it became physical. Carmen called Robert, and he called the police on his way to my house. When they arrived, they saw a scratch on me and took Carmen with them for questioning. Again that year, on June 19, Carmen and I were fighting. Someone called 911 and the police came and took Carmen away to the juvenile center since she had hurt me once again. I saw that she had been affected by the custody battle and was trying to act out the role of a parent. I did not blame her, certainly, and absolutely hated the fact that she was being taken away from me. It was the most traumatic experience I have had, imagining my baby in that awful place, having lost her to the system. No one in my whole family had ever gone to juvenile center or had even before a judge, and I was unprepared to deal with the heartbreaking nightmare of it. No mother gives birth to her child to see the day they are taken away by authorities because their parents made such a mess of their life. My heart was broken, and I was unable to sleep or eat, even work. Three days seemed like thirty years as I tried to save her from the assigned twenty-one-day juvenile center. I hired the best lawyer in the area, and I was able to get her out after three days and nights there. That was the beginning of my understanding Carmen, and she began to understand my point-of-view. It took us a couple of months to sort out everything with prayers and counseling. Carmen decided not to testify for the custody battle, and she decided to live with me. Robert dropped the custody battle two weeks before the trial date on September 7. Some times God brings us situations in our lives that are very heartbreaking, but they can be the beginning of blossoming and wholesome relationships.

An interesting thing about my culture is that in India there is no "age of adulthood," and the age of eighteen means nothing. Children stay with their parents until they are married, and people live together in families forever. The legal system makes no distinction for age, and parents take responsibility for their children no matter what mistakes they make. It is unfortunate that I had to learn the hard way how things are done in America, but praise God that Carmen was not yet considered an adult, and my lawyer and I were able to make things as easy on her as possible.

Due to legal implications, Carmen had to stay away from me and live with another family for a time. I was desperate, praying to God for her to be allowed to come home. I felt that I had lost someone I loved more than myself, and I saw her incredible potential that had been masked by her anger. In the end, my teenager was placed on nineteen-month probation, but due to the grace of God, it was reduced to only six months with community service, meaning that she would be completely free in February of 2006. On July 12, 2005, Carmen came home to live with me at last. She was so grateful for my help in shortening her sentence and for my unconditional love for her—I saw that her eyes were opened to how much I truly love my daughter. On July 16, 2005, Carmen, David, and

I went on a seven-day Alaskan cruise with TD Jakes Ministry, Holland America Cruise Line. We all three had a wonderful time. Before we left, I was unsure whether Carmen would be able to accompany us due to the court situation, but God made a way for Carmen to go. We reconnected as a family and made special memories. Carmen made some good friends as well. It was great to be together as a family. As we left Alaska for Florida, Carmen was in tears because she enjoyed her time so much and did not want to leave her new friends. Shortly after returning, Robert dropped the custody battle altogether and then I lost my job at the hospital, having taken too much personal time off dealing with legal issues. I decided to take a year off from working in order to reconnect with my kids, relax and de-stress, and seek direction from God for my future. In November, we were able to take another cruise to the Bahamas as a family. In spite of everything, God gave a wonderful time as a family.

During the probationary period, Robert came to me and asked me to forgive him and take him back as a husband. It was early December 2005, and he was desperate. He started to say intimate things to me about how I always liked his long neck and how he always wanted to make love to me. He said that he and I were certainly going to be man and wife one day again. This was right after the custody battle, the juvenile home, and the probation, and I was too overwhelmed by all of it to jump back into his arms. What were his motives? How could he go from sabotaging my relationship with the kids to wanting me back? I was still trying very hard to mend my relationship with my angry teenager, and we were going to counseling together and individually. I was praying constantly for God to help her work out her anger towards her parents and reconcile the two of us as mother and daughter. Earlier in the year, she and I even took a cruise together up in Alaska to have a fun time and reconnect with each other. I was paralyzed with the fear that Carmen would be taken from me again, that if Robert and I messed up and anything happened at all, I would lose my baby again. That was all I could think of at the time, and I did not want to hear the things Robert was saying. I practically ran away from him. Looking back, I wish things had been different that day, but I cannot live in a world of regret.

Robert became desperate to have a relationship with some-one. On July 5, he stopped by to see the kids and I saw a wed-ding band on his finger. Immediately, I shut down and would not let my emotions take over me. He wanted to talk about it, but I was not ready to say anything. It was like my heart was coming into my throat and I couldn't breathe. I simply told Robert that I was walking out the door to go somewhere and didn't have time to talk to him. He looked at me and said, "So you know?" and I still did not reply. It seemed that God had shut the door on my wish to be Robert's wife, and I knew that my life would take a 360-degree turn. I stood on Jeremiah 29:11, believing that God had plans to prosper me and not to harm me. That night I slept well and shed no tears. I trusted God's promise that He would not give me more than I could bear. Robert and I had an appointment to see my pastor later that month, and I cancelled it, knowing that I was still hurting about his remarriage and could not face him sitting there wear-ing that wedding ring. As much as he told me, he was sixty-three years old and needed financial and emotional security, health insurance, and that was why he married this woman, the fact remains that he married someone besides me. He said he had to do what he had to do.

Enough time passed that I once again forgave Robert and let him go. I still love him unconditionally and will be there for him whenever or wherever he needs me. He is the only man with whom I have ever had a long-term relationship, and he is my family, even closer than I was with my own parents. He is remarried and living his life, and I have let him go. My trust is in the will of God, and I continue to seek contentment despite how I might feel or what might happen to me circumstantially. I am getting back on my feet and preparing for a new era, one in which my children and I understand and respect each other in addition to me respecting myself. I have told Robert that he has my total forgiveness regarding the things he feels in his heart that he did to hurt me.

Now I am raising two teenagers, basically as a single parent with no grandparents' influence or father figure. I never dreamed I would be in this position, but I have learned to be there every moment that I can when David and Carmen are not with their friends or involved in some activity. Robert hardly sees the kids, being too busy with his new family. To be honest, our children don't care to see him much. I am available to them, and they depend on me to meet their physical, emotional, and spiritual needs. I watch David and Carmen feed the ducks in our backyard, play with our new puppy, argue with one another at times, show love to each other, and call me to ask, "What should I wear?" or, "Have you seen this commercial? I like this one." We enjoy watching television, such as "That 70s Show" and "Sponge Bob Squarepants." They are precious and a great blessing to me. I have come to realize that if I have eighty percent of the blessing I wished for in life, then I can't focus on the twenty percent I do not have. Instead, I am thankful for and concentrate on enjoying the eighty percent.

I am no longer the naïve East Indian girl who came to this country seeking the ideal life, but a woman who has been shaped by both circumstance and faith. I have been hurt, yes, but have forgiven those who injured me. I have been depressed and down but have learned to rely on God. I have been a good mom and a bad one, but I have learned to take it one day at a time. I have worked too much and then not worked at all, but I have learned that the people and relationships in life supersede any material interest. I have been saddened but have learned to find joy in the things of heaven. All of it is *life,* and thank you for taking the time to read what I've shared about mine.